FIVE BLUE HAIRED LADIES
SITTING ON A GREEN PARK BENCH

FIVE BLUE HAIRED LADIES
SITTING ON A GREEN PARK BENCH

by John A Penzotti

JOSEF WEINBERGER PLAYS

LONDON

First published in 2003
by Josef Weinberger Ltd
12-14 Mortimer Street, London, W1T 3JJ

ISBN 0 85676 268 7

Printed by Wrightson's, 2 & 3 Mallard Close, Earls Barton, Northants NN6 0JF.

FIVE BLUE HAIRED LADIES SITTING ON A GREEN PARK BENCH was first produced by Michael Rose Ltd and Chris Moreno Ltd at the Theatre Royal, Lincoln, on 6th March 2001. The cast was as follows:

GLADYS	Lynda Baron
LA LA	Miguel Brown
ROSE	Anne Charleston
EVA	Jean Fergusson
ANNA	Jennifer Wilson
SHIRLEY	Estelle Collins
TUFFY	Andrew Kwame
MARVIN	Harry Landis
NUNZIO	Gilbert Wynne
RICHARD/MAN	Simon Masterson-Smith

Two National UK tours of FIVE BLUE HAIRED LADIES SITTING ON A GREEN PARK BENCH followed during 2002 and 2003 with Shirley Anne Field (ANNA 2002), Carol Cleveland (ANNA 2003), Ruth Madoc (GLADYS 2002, 2003), Una Mclean (ROSE 2003), Hope Ross (EVA 2003) and Russell Hunter (MARVIN 2003).

Directed by Chris Colby

Staging by David Kort

Set design by Allan Miller-Bunford

Lighting design by Graham McLusky

Costume design by Amy MacNamara

To all the strong-willed, funny, passionate and bold women who have influenced my life over the years. I could not have written these words any better without your constant presence in mind, even if you have already passed on. Thank you.

ACT ONE

Scene One

Time: Whenever. Place: Washington Park Square. Setting:
Two benches, a large tree between them, sit centre stage. In
the distance behind it, silhouettes of other trees and a vague
New York City skyline splash across a scrim. Four older
women sit on the benches. We will come to learn that although
these women are from very different backgrounds, they share
common bonds, which have to do not only with where they
have been in their lives, but more importantly, where they are
going. They are: LA LA CARMICHAEL, *a Negro cabaret singer*
who only reached semi-fame in the 20s & 30s . . . planning a
comeback; ROSE O'CONNOR, *a spinster from Upstate New York*
who moved to the city after a brief stint as a WAC in the
service; EVA REISCH, *New York born and raised, married into*
high society, husband deceased, no children; GLADYS
FEINBERG, *married, separated, husband in a New Jersey rest*
home, two children, three grandchildren. Enter the fifth lady,
ANNA CINZANO, *four children, six grandchildren. Husband and*
four children are deceased, grandchildren have moved away.
She walks over to the bench, pulling a shopping cart behind
her. ANNA'S *face lights up, she's excited about something.*
Everyone focuses attention on her.

ANNA   Ooh, oh . . . (*She pauses, sighing.*) never mind,
                  I forgot.

                  (*Everyone goes back to mindless activity.*)

                  Wait . . . I remembered. (*Proudly.*) I had a Cool
                  Whip for the first time today.

                  (GLADYS *leans over from the other side of the*
                  bench.)

GLADYS   Big deal. I broke wind for the fifth time today.

                  (*The ladies shift away from* GLADYS.)

LA LA   I had sex.

(*Everyone turns and reacts, except for* ANNA, *who is still pondering Cool Whip.*)

ANNA   (*relishing the memory*) It was creamy, and white, and firm.

(*They turn to* ANNA.)

ANNA   The Cool Whip. It's freshness dated, ya know.

LA LA   September 23, 1948.

(*Everyone turns to* LA LA.)

The sex. It was 1948. He was a chorus boy. He claimed that he had sex with Josephine Baker . . . that bitch. If it were not for that banana-wearing bitty . . .

ANNA/ROSE/   We know, we know . . . 'You would have been a
EVA/GLADYS   star'.

LA LA   (*sardonically*) So I slept with him. I showed him a few tricks you could do with a banana that Jo Jo never thought of. (*Perplexed.*) He ran off with a stagehand shortly after the incident. Never really understood that?

ROSE   La La . . . you see those two men in the black leather jackets over there? Why don't you tell them that story and see what they say?

(GLADYS *clutches her handbag tightly.*)

GLADYS   They look like the kind of men who break into apartments and steal things.

ROSE   The only thing that they would steal are your Judy Garland records . . . and only after they've reupholstered your sofas, removed the plastic from the lamp shades and rearranged your knick knacks. They're gay.

EVA   Did you hear? Donald and Marla got divorced.
                   Such a shame. She really could have tried a
                   little harder.

ROSE   The man was cheating on her. It's not her fault
                   the marriage failed.

EVA   I'm not talking about the marriage. I'm talking
                   about the divorce settlement. I would not have
                   settled for anything less than forty million.

                   (ANNA *sits down.*)

ANNA   Which is why you're sitting on this park bench
                   with the rest of us today. Greed. Greed is a
                   terrible thing. Makes people ugly. Look at
                   Monica Lewinsky.

EVA   I'm sitting on this park bench with you because
                   I want to, not because I have nothing better to
                   do. I do, you know. I could be doing lots of
                   things right now. I just choose to be doing
                   this.

ROSE   And what might those things be? Shoe
                   shopping with Imelda Marcos? Picking out
                   wallpaper with Nancy Reagan? Or perhaps
                   planning a birthday party for Prince William.

LA LA   You'd better watch what you say to the first
                   lady over there, she'll rip off her tiara and beat
                   ya to death with it.

GLADYS   If she doesn't bore us to death with that damn
                   story about how she accidentally wandered
                   into the Lincoln bedroom and found Herbert
                   Hoover singing show tunes while wearing her
                   Black Velvet Patou Inaugural gown.

LA LA   I forgot, was it Rodgers and Hart, or Gershwin?

                   (EVA *stands up, walks over to* LA LA. *She
                   rummages through her purse, pulling out
                   photographs.*)

EVA   Look . . . look at these. This is a picture of me
              and Mamie Eisenhower . . . Me and Lady Bird
              Johnson . . . Me and Nancy Reagan. What have
              you got in your purse? A couple of old song
              sheets and some lint-covered mints? At least I
              was somebody . . . once, a long time ago . . .
              but I was somebody.

ROSE   Where's the one of you and Betty Ford? Oh, I
              forgot. They don't allow photographers at the
              clinic.

EVA   Bitch.

              (*Turning her back to the bench, moving
              towards the audience, she opens her purse and
              takes out a small leather folio. She carefully
              places the photographs into it, tying it closed.
              She places it back into her bag, takes a deep
              breath, returns to the bench. The women shift
              uncomfortably in their seats.*)

EVA   I'm sorry La La. I lost my head.

              (LA LA *fishes through her purse, pulls out the
              letter.*)

LA LA   You want to know what I have in my purse? A
              letter. The most important letter I have ever
              written in my life. (*Clearing her throat.*) Dear
              Mr William Morris. In lieu of the untimely and
              tragic death of Miss Josephine Baker, I feel
              that it is my duty to carry on the tradition
              which she has so richly laid.

GLADYS   (*aside*) Obviously she has not heard of the
              untimely and tragic death of Mr William Morris.

LA LA   I am offering you the chance to represent me in
              my comeback, further paving the way for, shall
              we say, ethnic songstresses everywhere. I will
              be appearing at the Rainbow and Stars on the
              twentieth and twenty sixth of this month and

have reserved a table for you on both nights.
Until we meet . . . sincerely yours, La La
Carmichael.

ROSE   Hang on a minute . . .

LA LA   PS: Feel free to bring a contract with you.

ROSE   How did you get a gig at Rainbow and Stars?

LA LA   Well, I haven't yet . . . but I will. I sent them
one of my 78s. They'll call. I got a feeling . . .
(*Touching her heart.*) Right here.

GLADYS   It's probably Angina.

(ANNA *fishes through her purse.*)

ANNA   I got a letter today.

EVA   From your grandchildren?

(ANNA *pulls out the letter.*)

ANNA   No. From Ed McMahan. You may have already
won ten million dollars.

(ROSE *throws her hands up in the air.*)

ROSE   You may have also already died and gone to
Heaven. (*Looking around.*) In which case,
Sister Mary Denise has a lot of explaining to
do.

(GLADYS *rises from the bench, starts gathering
herself together.*)

GLADYS   I have to go now, I'm tired.

ANNA   You've been tired a lot lately.

GLADYS   I know. My grandchildren are coming for
dinner. I have to get ready.

ROSE   They only visit for one reason. To convince
                you to go to a home. Every month they come
                by and try and guilt you into reconciling with
                Marvin and moving to that prison rest home in
                New Jersey. And why? Because then they can
                come and visit, drain your cheque books and
                not have to worry if you fall and break a hip,
                because some Nurse Ratchett will be there to
                pick you up.

ANNA   I read somewhere once that you don't fall and
                break a hip. You break a hip and then you fall.

ROSE   Which brings me back to my original point. If a
                grandparent falls in a rest home and there are
                no grandchildren around to hear, do they feel
                guilty?

GLADYS   What a terrible, and stupid, thing to say. My
                grandchildren are very concerned about me and
                love me very much. And I'm sorry if that makes
                you jealous and bitter.

LA LA   Oh, that doesn't make her jealous and bitter.
                Having never had a man in her life. That makes
                her bitter.

ANNA   What do you mean? Rosy the Rivetter here
                probably had a whole army of men around
                during the war.

LA LA   What was wrong there? Couldn't find one with
                a big enough bayonet?

                (ROSE *goes into her purse and pulls out a pack
                of cigarettes and a lighter, lights up.*)

GLADYS   Those things could kill you Rose. You know
                that, don't ya?

ROSE   I'm old, Gladys. A feta cheese omelette could
                kill me just as easily. Besides, there are a lot of
                worse things in this world that I could be

sticking in my mouth. Pot . . . pills . . . (*To*
ANNA.) Cool Whip!

EVA   Someone followed me here. I know it. Yesterday
when I was on my way home, I saw him. He's
been following me for days.

ROSE   It's your overactive imagination. You're
paranoid.

EVA   No. I'm not. When I got home I put a piece of
tape over the listen button on my intercom.
That way I could hear everyone coming and
going in the building. I heard him, standing in
the hall.

ANNA   So, what happened?

EVA   He went away. I think he's from the Mob.

ROSE   There is no Mob on the Upper East Side, Eva.
Just Yuppies.

(GLADYS *moves around the back of the bench,
creeping up on* EVA.)

ANNA   Where is he now?

EVA   He's here. I can feel it.

(GLADYS *places her hand on* EVA's *shoulder.*
EVA *is startled.*)

GLADYS   (*spooky voice*) Eva, Eva. Where's my golden
arm?

(*Everyone starts laughing.* EVA *is upset.*)

EVA   When they find me dead in the basement of my
building, you'll be sorry.

GLADYS   When they find you dead in the basement of
your building? When they find you dead in the
basement of your building? Is that anyway to

talk? Eva, you really think about the most God-awful things, don't you?

EVA

What do you expect? I'm an old woman, living all alone in New York City. I have no husband, no children. No one.

ROSE

You have all of us.

ANNA

And that's more than a lot of people have. Have you ever walked down the street and seen how many people are alone?

LA LA

They could just be walking alone. They're not necessarily alone.

ANNA

No, they're alone. You can see it in their eyes. Imagine, a city chock-full of wonderful people, and millions of them are all alone.

GLADYS

Why do you think that is?

ANNA

Because they are afraid. Afraid to talk to strangers.

EVA

Why do you think they call them strangers? They're strange.

GLADYS

Well . . . one night when I was coming home from the senior centre I was waiting for my bus. It was rainy and damp, the chill went right to my bones. There was only this young woman waiting, so I wasn't too scared . . . we stood, not saying a word, and then this homeless woman came over to us. She tried to start a conversation with the young woman. I immediately started reading my magazine. She frightened me.

EVA

Smart woman. You never know what they'll do.

GLADYS

I listened to her, she seemed harmless. But the woman waiting for the bus wanted no part of her.

ANNA   What did she want?

GLADYS   She wanted money for a cup of coffee. She had
          a transfer for the bus and she was bargaining
          with the woman, telling her that the transfer
          was worth fifty cents and she asked her to
          purchase it from her for that amount.

EVA   Did she?

GLADYS   No. She ignored the old woman. There stood
          this young woman, dressed in her fine blue
          suit, with her polished leather shoes, and then
          there was this withered old woman, in a torn
          sweater, plastic bags over her shoes, and I
          thought to myself, I was once that young
          woman, and now the only difference between
          me and that old woman is a social security
          cheque. Well, she came over to me and offered
          up the wrinkled transfer. I looked into her eyes,
          I took the transfer, and gave her five quarters.
          Then she did the strangest thing. She took two
          of the quarters and put them into her pocket,
          and handed me back the other three.

ANNA   Good heavens, what for?

GLADYS   She said to me, the transfer is worth fifty cents,
          and fifty cents is all I expect.

EVA   You think she would have pocketed the rest for
          later.

GLADYS   She may not have had much but she still had
          self-esteem and a sense of honesty. When she
          smiled at me as she walked off, suddenly that
          chill in the air was gone. Well, the bus pulled
          up, and as the younger woman got on she
          looked at me. We both learned something that
          night. And I hope that neither one of us ever
          forgets.

(GLADYS prepares to leave. ANNA also gathers her things.)

ANNA
Come on, I'll walk with you. I have a gun in my purse. No leather thug will bother us.

ROSE
Where did you get a gun? They wouldn't give you a driver's license, but they gave you a gun permit?

ANNA
My grandson gave it to me before he moved to Florida. I didn't want to take it, but then he told me that Sylvester Stallone's mother carries one.

EVA
Sylvester Stallone's mother also wears sparkling blue eye shadow, gold lame headbands and talks to the dead.

(ANNA takes GLADYS by the arm, grabs her shopping cart.)

ANNA
Don't listen to them, Gladys. Besides, there are no bullets in the gun. I took them out one day while I was cleaning it. I forgot where I put them. They'll turn up.

(ANNA and GLADYS exit, stage left.)

LA LA
There they go . . . Thelma and Louise of Beekman Place.

EVA
A gun. She has a gun and I'm paranoid. What's wrong with this picture? I feel for Gladys. Rose, ya know everyone is not out to get your money, and it's not right of you to assume that her grandchildren only want her around for her money. How do you think that makes her feel? Just cause we're old doesn't mean we have nothing to give. We do.

ROSE
What? What do we have to give? Why do we have to be the ones doing the giving? We've been giving all our lives, now we're made to

feel like we're taking up space. People wait for us to die so that they can get our three hundred dollar a month rent-controlled apartment. When you get on the subway, or the bus, we have priority seating. Don't you think that for one minute there is not someone, like that young woman at the bus stop, who would rather be sitting in the seat near the door? Do they ever stop and think that one of us, or someone like us who was young once, designed that building that they're living in? Or the road that they drive on? I don't envy Gladys. As far as I'm concerned I have one person in my life that will look out for me and you're looking at her.

LA LA   No wonder you walk crooked. That chip on your shoulder must be awful heavy.

ROSE   Dead straight, and it's not made of chocolate either.

EVA   No. She's right. I know just how she feels. I see it, I hear it. When I'm walking down the street and some young kid brushes past me. Not that it was intentional that they bumped into me, but suddenly and only for a moment or two, I still feel like I was in the way. And then I feel like saying, I'm sorry, I didn't realize I had veered out of the slow lane into the express lane. And then I'll watch as they get further and faster and I wonder, 'where could you be going in that big of a hurry'. I swear, sometimes I feel like the entire city has a chronic tardiness problem and everyone is always five to ten minutes late. And just because I am not moving at the speed of light, doesn't mean that I have nowhere to go or nothing to do. So, who cares if I spend three hours deciding between a sheer, or sandalfoot or . . . or between nude and beige? Maybe it's all I've got to do.

(Rose *and* La La *stare at her in manic state. Quietly,* Rose *reaches into her pocket.*)

ROSE   Eva! Here . . . (*Tossing her a small RX bottle.*) You need that more than I do.

EVA   What is it?

ROSE   Valium.

(La La *chuckles,* Eva *huffs. Blackout.*)

Scene Two

Time: A couple of days later. Place: The bench. Setting: Eva, La La *and* Rose *sit on the bench.*

EVA   Gladys isn't coming today.

ROSE   Those kids probably wore her out.

EVA   Children, what a nice thought.

LA LA   It's a little late for that nice thought now, Eva.

EVA   Oh, I know. But still. I have a confession to make. Last week I went into a card store and bought a condolence card for Marie Tommesetti and as I passed the section with the picture frames I saw this little ceramic one with a giraffe and a teddy bear on it. And inside was a photo of these two sweet looking children. I bought it, took it home and put it on the mantle.

ROSE   You're supposed to take that picture out and put one of your own in there . . . Brainiac.

EVA   I know that, Rose. But I don't have a picture to put in there. And I don't have any memories up here either. (*Pointing at her head.*)

LA LA	You keep doing things like that and people will think there ain't nothing up there.
ROSE	Didn't you and Richard try and have children?
EVA	Oh, we tried. And I was going to have a child. But I lost it in the fourth month. It was very hard on us. We had been married five years and he really wanted children, but after this happened we were afraid. I was more afraid than he was. I felt like something was wrong with me and I was right. When I went to the doctor he told me that I would never be able to have a child. Or if I did the chances would be that there would be something terribly wrong with it. I never told Richard about the visit to the doctor. After a while we got caught up in our lives, going to fancy parties and social events and the void seemed to be filled. We resolved ourselves to the fact that there would never be a child.
LA LA	You could have adopted.
EVA	We did. His name was Willy. (*She beams with a big smile, remembering.*) He was just two months old when we got him.
ROSE	Through an agency?
EVA	The ASPCA.
LA LA	What?
ROSE	(*sighs*) Dear God . . .
EVA	Willy was my little terrier. He was adorable and my best friend in the world. They say man's best friend, but I know better. He kept me company on all those nights when Richard would work late or go out of town. Outlived Richard by four years. He lost control of his kidneys and I had him put to sleep.

LA LA   You put your husband to sleep?

EVA   No. The dog. Sometimes I wished I could have
               put Richard to sleep. I used to call him Willy
               Wee Wee till I found out what was wrong with
               him. I thought he was just so happy to see me,
               that he tinkled on the floor.

ROSE   How did you lose Richard?

EVA   I was in Bergdorf Goodman and he wandered
               off . . .

ROSE   No. How did he die?

EVA   That's what I am telling you . . . we were in
               Bergdorf Goodman and he wandered off while I
               was trying on a dress. When I came out of the
               fitting room to have him zip me up I couldn't
               find him and there was all this commotion at
               the other end of the hall in the shoe
               department. I ran over, half-zipped in this ball
               gown and there was Richard, slumped over a
               chair, clutching the most beautiful, elegant,
               strappy sandal in his hand. Dead.

LA LA   What did you do?

EVA   I bought the shoes, wore them to his funeral.
               (*Sigh.*) To this day I have trouble walking into
               Bergdorf's in springtime.

               (ANNA *enters.*)

ANNA   What are you talking about?

EVA   Shoes.

ROSE   Death.

LA LA   And dogs.

ANNA   Sounds like an interesting conversation.
               Where's Gladys?

EVA	She's not coming.
ROSE	So, what have you got for us today? Macadainias, or Mace?
ANNA	Nothing. My cheque didn't come so I have to wait til tomorrow to go to the store. It's okay. Chef Boyardee will see to dinner tonight.
EVA	That's kids' food.
ROSE	Look who's eating it?
EVA	There are so many preservatives and sodium in those canned foods.
ROSE	Oh, everything has stuff in it. Lord knows what they're shooting into chickens these days. The poor things are probably junkies by the time they die.
EVA	Well, I try and eat healthy so I'll live longer.
ROSE	Longer than what? A can of ravioli?
EVA	No. But I'm not going to smoke myself into an early grave. Thank goodness that I'm a healthy, vibrant woman.
LA LA	(*to herself*) The last time I was healthy and vibrant I had a glass of champagne in one hand and Harry Belafonte's balls in the other. (*Everyone looks. She looks back, ashamed and aghast.*) Did I say that out loud?
EVA	I can't believe you said it at all. You did not sleep with Harry Belafonte.
LA LA	Well, I don't have pictures to prove it the way you do. Besides, a lady never kisses and tells.
EVA	No. But she'll accept all jewellery freely.

ANNA   How did we manage to go from dogs, to death,
              to shoes, to Harry Belafonte's genitalia all in
              one day? Whoever said old people have
              nothing to say sure never sat on this bench.

EVA   I think I'll go to visit Richard. I like to go and
              polish the little marble cameo on the
              headstone. It's kind of like straightening his tie
              before he walks out the door, or fixing that one
              cuff link that was always turned sideways. (EVA
              rises to leave.)

ANNA   (*smiling*) Or clipping his nose hairs before they
              got so long you could braid them.

              (*At first* EVA *is appalled by the 'low' comment.
              Then she realizes its sincerity. She smiles at*
              ANNA *and they share a moment.*)

EVA   Well . . . yes. I guess you're right.

              (*She kisses* ANNA *on the cheek and exits.
              Lights fade to black.*)

                         Scene Three

Time: Afternoon, the next day. Place: The bench. Setting:
ROSE, LA LA *and* GLADYS *sit on the bench.* GLADYS *has a*
crossword puzzle book. Enter ANNA *pulling her shopping cart.*

ANNA   Where's Eva?

LA LA   Never showed up.

ROSE   Maybe the bogeyman got her.

              (ANNA *sits down on the bench, rummaging
              through her shopping cart.*)

ANNA   Well she's gonna miss out. Guess what I have?

ROSE   A hand grenade?

GLADYS   Vermin.

                (ANNA *turns to* GLADYS.)

ANNA   What?

GLADYS   Vermin. A six letter word for rodent. Vermin.

ANNA   Pringles potato chips.

                (ANNA *produces the canister of chips from her bag.*)

ROSE   What are you doing? Why are you buying this crap?

ANNA   Rose. Let me tell you something. For twenty years I never set foot in a grocery store. Nunzio and I ate out every night. Now that he's gone, I cook for myself. One day while I was in the grocery store I realized just how many things I have never tried. Like Cool Whip. Look at this . . .

GLADYS   There are a lot of things in this world that I'm curious about, but I'm a little too old to try them now.

                (ANNA *stares into the canister, amazed.*)

ANNA   How many chips do you think are in there?

ROSE   Enough to clog the one and only artery you've got left. Give me those, before you hurt yourself.

                (ANNA *and* ROSE *start fighting over the chips. The canister goes flying over the bench, chips everywhere.*)

ANNA   (*angry*) You owe me two dollars and forty nine cents.

GLADYS   Fetus.

LA LA   Excuse me?

GLADYS   Fetus. A five letter word for an unborn child.
                Fetus.

LA LA   Gladys. What is the point of doing a crossword
                puzzle?

GLADYS   It keeps my mind sharp. Where is Eva? She's
                always good at these.

ROSE   Especially if they're about the Royal Family or
                Melrose Place.

ANNA   You should really be gentler to Eva. She's had
                a hard life. Things really fell apart after her
                husband died. The government took all their
                money. I don't think she's ever adjusted. Did
                you know that her husband embezzled money
                from the government so that he could pay for
                his mistress? Imagine that, your husband dies
                and this woman shows up, demanding money. I
                sometimes lay awake at night and wonder how
                someone could do such a thing.

                (ROSE *stares off into the sky.*)

ROSE   Darkness is anxiety's magnifying glass.
                Everything seems worse in the dark. Sometimes
                it's not much better in the morning. But you've
                just got to thank God that you got to see the
                morning and go on.

LA LA   After seven months of coming to this bench
                day in and day out Rose O'Connor, this is the
                first time I have heard you mention God.

ROSE   Well just because I don't mention it all the
                time, doesn't mean I don't believe it.

                (*A young couple, very punk-looking, walks by
                the bench. There sex is unclear. They stop in
                front of the ladies and kiss. They smile. Then*

*they walk on, hand in hand. NB: this is
indicated by the ladies looking at them and
reacting to the situation. No actors needed.)*

ANNA   What in the name of Heaven was that?

ROSE   Young Love. (*She sighs.*)

LA LA   Girls dressed like boys, boys dressed like girls.
Why is it that no one wants to look like who
they are any more?

ROSE   I think it's okay for them to be whatever they
want to be. We never had that luxury. We
spent the first two decades of our lives
growing into what our parents wanted us to be.
And then we spent the next decade undoing all
of it in order to become what we truly are.
Thirty some-odd years down the drain. And the
next twenty years catching up and mending
ourselves to a point where we could stand up
and be happy and proud. All because we
needed to give our parents that sense of
accomplishment. But where was ours?

GLADYS   Identity. An eight letter word that defines who
we are. There, it's finished.

LA LA   Do you think Eva is okay? I would hate to think
that she was right about being followed.

ROSE   She's just a silly old woman.

LA LA   And what are we? Spice Girls?

ROSE   Listen. When my time comes, I'll go quietly,
without a sound and without fear. After all.
We've been on this planet a long time. We've
seen a lot of things.

LA LA   (*proudly*) Some of us more than others.

ROSE   All I'm saying is, when it's time, it's time. And
it's no one's decision but you-know-who's.

ANNA   That's twice in one day. What brought this on?

ROSE   I was watching the TV the other day. It was
           one of my favourite movies. *The Little
           Princess,* with Shirley Temple. It was so
           beautiful. When it was over I was in tears. Her
           father sitting in that chair. (*She mimics the
           film.*) Sarah . . . Sarah. It was so heart-warming.
           Suddenly, right after the credits . . . *Fox Five
           News.* An infant is found dead in a New Jersey
           hotel room. Bam. Reality strikes again. And I
           sat there. And I thought to myself, 'Why?'
           Then it came to me. Sometimes the dreams of
           life are interrupted by the alarm clock of reality.

LA LA   Like, just after the stable boy has thrown you
           down in the hay, but just before he rips off his
           shirt.

ROSE   No, I mean time is short, and life is fleeting,
           and . . .

ANNA   A stitch in time saves nine.

ROSE   No. I mean, oh, forget it. Forget it.

ANNA   I'm sorry Rose, go on.

ROSE   It's not what you are. It's what you do and
           who you share it with. I read somewhere that
           it's not what you experience in life that counts,
           it's what you learn from those experiences.

GLADYS   So what did you learn?

ROSE   I learned that there are a lot of screwed up
           people in this world and you never know who's
           crazy and who's not. I'm going home to call
           Eva.

           (ROSE *gets up. Gathers herself together, kisses*
           LA LA *and* GLADYS *on the cheek.*)

ROSE   (*as she kisses* ANNA) Stop buying crap, okay? (*She turns before leaving.*) I'll see you soon.

(ROSE *exits.*)

GLADYS   What the hell was that all about?

ANNA   Oh, you know how she gets all melancholy around D-Day. The war was all she really had. That and her friend Shirley. When Shirley passed on a couple of years ago it was quite a blow.

LA LA   It's all tragedy, I'll admit. We've all lost dear friends over the years. But it's not like she lost her husband.

ANNA   No, she lost her wife.

(GLADYS *and* LA LA *look at her perplexed.* ANNA *nods, raising an eyebrow.*)

GLADYS   What do you mean wife? She's a . . . and you can't have a . . . unless.

LA LA   Unless you're a . . .

(ANNA *nods and raises an eyebrow again.*)

ANNA   Member of the church. Friend of Dorothy.

GLADYS   Dorothy who?

LA LA   Are you saying that Rose is a homo-sectional?

ANNA   No dear. That would mean that she's a large gay sofa. She's a lesbian.

LA LA   How do you know?

GLADYS   Did you???

ANNA   No. NEVER. I was at Shirley's funeral. I saw the way that Rose looked at the coffin. I could see

in her eyes that she had not just lost a friend. I
could see myself in her eyes. It was just the
same way that I looked the day I lost Nunzio.
But it was even worse. There was Rose,
surrounded by Shirley's family. Brothers,
sisters, cousins. All of them never realized a
thing. They lamented how Shirley had never
shared the joy of a husband and children. Then
I saw Rose . . . standing at the buffet table. She
was paler than cottage cheese on a fruit plate. I
thought she was going to burst. I took her into
the next room and sat her down. I found myself
consoling her, saying things to her that I had
heard only two years before . . . 'You made her
happy for so many years . . . She would not
want you to give up the rest of your life'. All
the while she looked at me I thought, 'it
doesn't matter who you love. You have loved
and been loved'. It may be the one thing in life
that we can take with us to our graves.

(GLADYS *and* LA LA *sit pondering* ANNA'S
words as the stage falls slowly dark.)

Scene Four

Time: The very next day. Place: The bench. Setting: ROSE,
GLADYS *and* LA LA *sit on the bench. No one is talking. There is
tension in the air.* LA LA *has her back to* ROSE, *foot tapping.*

LA LA   (*angry*) Why didn't you tell us you were gay?

ROSE   Cause you never asked.

GLADYS   Well, why would we ask? We just assumed
               that . . .

ROSE   Well what was I supposed to say? Hey, check
               out the babe over by the water fountain. Nice
               tits. I mean, does it matter?

GLADYS   Well, no.

LA LA   (*a bit huffy*) What do you mean no? Of course it matters. It's a part of your life. Just like my singing and Gladys' grandchildren, Eva's paranoia and Anna's fixation with freeze-dried food. We share things with each other every day. And I, for one, am hurt.

GLADYS   What's it like?

ROSE   Excuse me?

GLADYS   No, not that. No, I don't need to know about that. I mean, keeping it a secret. Anna told us about Shirley's funeral. How awful for you.

ROSE   Do you want to see a picture of her?

                     (ROSE *pulls a locket out from around her neck. She opens it, smiling at the photo. She shows it to* GLADYS *and* LA LA.)

GLADYS   How did she . . .

ROSE   She was mugged on her way home from a party. These animals evidently saw us kissing good night on the corner of Seventh Avenue and Charles Street. I was on my way to a friends uptown and she was heading home. After we said our goodbyes, they followed behind her and started to harass her as she walked down the street. I found a message on the machine from the emergency room when I got home. I rushed right over there. Walking into that hospital I had the most awful feeling I have ever had in my life. Two hours later she was gone. Before she died, she told me what had happened . . . what they said to her as they kicked her and spat on her and then Shirley told me that she loved me and she thanked me for making her richer in love than she had ever dreamed possible. And I thought to myself, because I loved you so much that I didn't care if the world knew, you have died. Was I selfish? Was I wrong? Or was everyone else

wrong because they just looked at us and not
inside of us to see the real meaning of that
kiss. And that is why I never told you. That is
why I have never told a soul after that. But
Anna, Anna knew. And now you know, too.

(GLADYS *moves closer to* ROSE, *taking her*
hand.)

GLADYS   From now on, you come to us with anything
that makes your heart heavy. That's what we're
here for. That's what this bench is for. Support.

(ANNA, *riding micro-scooter, goes flying past*
the bench, bag on tow shouting 'WAASSUP'.
The ladies notice. A loud crash offstage. The
ladies react. A moment later ANNA *appears.*)

ANNA   Thank God for the garbage strike. I might have
been road pizza if it weren't for those hefty
bags.

ROSE   Anna May Cinzano, have you lost your mind?
You could have fallen and broken a hip.

ANNA   I told you, you don't fall and break a hip, you
break a hip and then you fall.

ROSE   Oh, then by all means, sign me up for the
Annual Bungee Jump off the GW Bridge. Sit
down on this bench before I kill you myself, I
have a bone to pick with you.

(ANNA *looks at* GLADYS *and* LA LA, *they shrug.*
ANNA *sits down.*)

ANNA   I know what you're going to say.

ROSE   Why did you . . .

ANNA   It's okay. (*She opens her bag and pulls out a*
can of reduced-fat Pringles.) See? Reduced-fat.
However, there is the matter of two dollars and
forty-nine cents.

ROSE   Let's talk about the matter of spilling the beans
            about my private life.

ANNA   Oh, that. Well, come on Rose, look around you.
            It's the 21st century. Get with it. Even Ellen
            DeGeneres did it.

GLADYS   We told you it doesn't matter.

ROSE   Well it does to me. What if you didn't take the
            news well? What then?

LA LA   Lets face it, we're all too old to play the game,
            but there's nothing wrong with throwing the
            dice once in a while to see what comes up.
            Could be your lucky seven, could be snake
            eyes.

ANNA   Eeuuh, I hate snakes. One time there was one in
            my garden and Nunzio took the shovel and
            chopped its head off. (*Remembering.*) He was
            my knight in shining armour.

GLADYS   Well, if you plan on riding that scooter again, I
            suggest you borrow that armour.

ANNA   Oh, I won't be doing that again. It was just a
            one-time thing. The young man who lives
            downstairs from me just broke up with his
            girlfriend and he was throwing some things
            away and I saw it lying there in the hall and I
            figured, well . . . it's better to try it, than
            wonder what it's all about.

ROSE   So what's it all about?

ANNA   Sheer terror. At first it was fun, then there came
            the hill and, well, I'll tell you, that thing can
            cure Alzheimer's.

LA LA   What?

ANNA   My entire life flashed in front of my eyes. (*All laugh.*)

LA LA   Hey Gladys, how was the visit from your grandchildren?

ROSE   Did you count the silver after they left?

GLADYS   Actually smarty-pants, they bought me a present.

              (GLADYS *reaches under her blouse and produces a chain with a Medic Alert panic button on the end of it.*)

GLADYS   A Lifecall Medic Alert panic button. This way they won't have to worry about me being alone.

              (ROSE *starts laughing, falls into* LA LA'S *lap.*)

ROSE   Gladys, Gladys, help I've fallen and I can't get up.

LA LA   (*laughing*) Push the button! Push the button!

GLADYS   Very funny.

ANNA   I think it was a nice gesture.

LA LA   Well, I think it's silly. You're gonna start walking around with that thing in your hand waiting for something bad to happen.

ROSE   She'll probably wear it in the shower and electrocute herself with it. Bzzzzz. (ROSE *and* LA LA *laugh,* ANNA *blushes.*)

GLADYS   I don't have to sit here and take this, I'm leaving.

              (GLADYS *gathers her things and exits.*)

ROSE   And drinking . . .

LA LA   It's eleven O'clock in the morning!

ROSE   It's that late already?

ANNA   I have four more in my bag. You want one?

                (LA LA *sits down on the bench. She shakes her
                head in disgust.* ANNA *digs out another
                bottle.*)

LA LA   It's the devil's brew.

ANNA   Actually, it's Raspberry Burst. They were out
                of Devil's Brew . . . lighten up, sister.

                (LA LA *accepts the bottle from* ANNA, *pops off
                the top.*)

LA LA   I haven't had a drink in years. I left my
                husband because of this stuff. He would get all
                liquored up and . . . you know.

GLADYS   Beat you?

LA LA   No. Cheat on me. The louse. (*She pauses,
                thinking.*) Well, it is a bit warm out here today,
                what's a little gonna hurt?

                (*She takes a sip, looks at the label, then
                proceeds to down the entire contents.*)

ROSE   You certainly fell off that high horse awfully
                fast.

ANNA   Want some Cheese Whiz?

ROSE   Cheese what?

GLADYS   Cheese Whiz. Even I've had Cheese Whiz.
                Break it out, Cinzano.

(ANNA *pulls the can of Cheese Whiz out of her handbag, handing it to* GLADYS.)

ANNA   Here you go. Did you know this has a shelf life of seventy-five years?

GLADYS   All right factoid, where are the crackers?

ANNA   Crackers? You eat it with crackers?

ROSE   You don't eat it with crackers? What do you put it on?

ANNA   My finger. Watch.

(ANNA *puts Cheese Whiz along her finger, concentrating very hard on not spilling it, as she is getting tipsy. She sticks her finger in her mouth, sighs. She goes to hand the can to* GLADYS.)

GLADYS   I'll pass.

(ANNA *offers it to* ROSE *and* LA LA *who decline also. She puts the can back in her bag.*)

ANNA   (*a bit flustered*) I know you eat it with crackers. I forgot them. I forget a lot of things lately. I can't remember what I had for breakfast. Some days I can't remember if I checked the mailbox and check it two, three times, even after I've got the mail. I'll walk out to the box and when I get back, there it is in the hall . . . the mail. I mean, I can remember, vividly, the dress I wore the night they gave Nunzio the Businessman of the Year award in 1947, but I can't remember if I ate breakfast. I don't understand.

LA LA   It's only natural. You're getting older. We all are. Don't you think we all forget things?

ROSE   And sometimes there are things we wish we could forget. But you remember the important things, like Nunzio.

LA LA	Hell, one day I forgot to put on underwear. I didn't realize it till I walked out of the door and good old Jack Frost gave me a wedgy. There's no harm in forgetting.
ANNA	Oh no! I forgot again! I was supposed to have blood drawn today. (*Passing out the wine coolers as she heads out. First* GLADYS, *then* ROSE.) The last round is on me.
LA LA	Why? All they're gonna find is Cheese Wiz, wine coolers and chips.
ANNA	(*handling a bottle to* LA LA *with a snicker*) Ya know La La dear, sarcasm is an ugly emotion on you . . . come to think of it, so is that coat.
	(*She exits.* LA LA *buffs at the comment. They crack open the bottles and toast each other.*)
GLADYS	Oh, forget her, she's drunk.
LA LA	Charlie. There's someone worth forgetting. We were only married for three months when he told me to give up my career and move back to Idaho with him.
GLADYS	He told you! You don't strike me as someone who can be told what to do.
LA LA	We were having some problems. What with me out till all hours every night singing and what not. And I would come home and there he'd be in his chair.
GLADYS	Didn't he come to see you sing?
LA LA	He would come once in a while. At first. But then he stopped coming all together. He would just sit home in his chair, watching TV. Or so I thought. I remember one night I came home and I was very upset. We'd had a fight before I left that evening and in the middle of *Love Don't*

Love You No More, I started to lose my voice and I froze. I couldn't remember the words and walked off stage. Well, I returned moments later and started to sing again.

GLADYS

Weren't you scared?

(ROSE *begins to quietly nod off.* LA LA *continues.*)

LA LA

Scared to death. But I got through it. I came home and told Charlie what happened. He said it was the beginning of the end. He wasn't supportive at all. He said, 'If you don't got what it takes, take it and go'. I started thinking maybe he was right. I went into the kitchen to make myself a drink and when I opened up the liquor cabinet, which was always stocked, I found one lone bottle, half empty, sitting there. I finally figured out what Charlie did every night while I was out there trying to make a name for myself and a life for the two of us.

GLADYS

When did you find out he was cheating?

LA LA

During the argument he told me that he was having an affair with Doris Hoffsteder from down the hall. Then he tried to tell me that my voice wasn't the only thing that I was losing. That's when he told me to move back to Idaho with him, so he could sell cars with his cousin Fred, or else. I filed for divorce two weeks later.

GLADYS

He wanted you to be a housewife?

LA LA

Yeah. Could you see me as a housewife? I told him that I was born to sing in front of crowds of people and not sinks full of dishes.

GLADYS

I could see you as a housewife. Just like I could see Rosie here with a feather duster, pearls and an apron.

(*She nudges* ROSE, *who falls over onto* LALA's *lap. Her handbag and the empty wine cooler bottle falls to the ground – she is passed out cold.* GLADYS *and* LA LA *look at each other in shock. There is a tense moment of silence, then panic ensues.*)

GLADYS   Oh my God, she's dead!!!

(GLADYS *grabs her panic button and starts pressing it furiously. Then she starts shrieking into it as if it were a walkie-talkie.*)

GLADYS   Help! Help! Dead lesbian in Washington Square Park.

(LA LA g*ently smacks* ROSE *on the cheek, trying to revive her. Nothing happens. She becomes nervous and her leg starts shaking.*)

LA LA   (*singing*) Amazing Grace, how sweet the sound . . .

GLADYS   411!! 411!!

(ROSE'S *head starts bouncing up and down on* LA LA's *knee.* ROSE, *disorientated, wakes with a start.*)

ROSE   AIR RAID!!! Sound the alarms! Incoming! Incoming!

GLADYS   Oh thank God. We thought you had . . .

LA LA   . . . Kicked the bucket.

ROSE   Oh my head. Does anyone have any asprin?

GLADYS   Ya got a headache?

ROSE   No, I'm teething. Between the Hooch and a Hop-along Carmichael here, I feel like my head's gonna explode.

LA LA   Devil's brew. I told you it was the Devil's brew.

               (*They gather their things and help a weary*
               ROSE *up..*)

GLADYS   We'll get some on the way home. I think we
               should leave before the ambulance shows up.

               (*They laugh as they start offstage. Blackout.*)

Scene Six

Time: Late afternoon. One week later. Place: The bench.
Setting: The stage lights come up revealing GLADYS *sitting on*
the bench drinking a cup of coffee. We hear birds singing in
the distance. She looks around.

GLADYS   Ya know Marvin, you just can't tell what's
               going to happen next these days. I wish you
               weren't so clueless. For thirty years we were
               together and every morning you offered me
               milk for my coffee and for thirty years every
               morning I said, 'No thank you'. We all make
               choices, Marvin. I know you're happy in that
               home. You have your TV, a comfy chair and a
               bunch of cronies to play cards with. That world
               isn't big enough for me. (*A beat.*) I may not
               have much, my crossword puzzles, my friends
               and a bench that's harder than a Rhino's butt
               but I still have options. So we aren't young
               any more. But that doesn't mean we need to get
               out of the race. We just join a slower race. But
               you just wanted to hang up your running
               shoes altogether, sit in front of a television and
               watch the rest of the world go by. Now,
               sometimes I don't do much more than that but
               at least I'm on the inside looking out, not
               outside looking in. I want to find things out for
               myself, make my own choices. (*Holding up her*
               coffee cup to the sky.) I drink my coffee black,
               Marvin. I always have and always will. I never
               told you flat out, and you never got the hint. I
               guess that's the difference. You choose to live

with your eyes wide open and your mind shut
tight. I can't look and not see. Sometimes I
wish I could. But I can't. Do I love you? Yes.
Oh, we'll end up together again eventually,
we'll probably be spending eternity together.
So what's a few years in separate bedrooms
beforehand?

(LA LA *enters.*)

LA LA	Who are you talking to?
GLADYS	(*looking up*) Marvin.
LA LA	He's in New Jersey, Gladys, not heaven. I don't think he can hear you.
GLADYS	I know. Have you heard from Anna today?
LA LA	No. Haven't heard from Eva or Rose either. And no, I haven't heard from William Morris. (*Bitter.*) Thanks for asking.
GLADYS	La La. I have something to tell you. (*Long Pause.*) William Morris is dead. He died a long time ago. Hence, I don't think you will be receiving a letter from him.
LA LA	What? When did this happen?
GLADYS	About twenty years ago.
LA LA	So why didn't any of you tell me? I might as well have addressed that letter to Santa Claus.

(LA LA *sits, disappointed and delusioned.*)

GLADYS	We didn't tell you because we thought you would just let it pass. But since you didn't and since no one else is here to break it to you, well . . . there are worse things that I could have told you.
LA LA	Well, no matter. I'll just write to Ed Sullivan.

GLADYS   Dead.

LA LA   Lawrence Welk!

GLADYS   Dead.

LA LA   Glenn Miller!

GLADYS   Dead.

LA LA   Duke Ellington!

GLADYS   Dead.

LA LA   Benny Goodman?

GLADYS   Dead.

LA LA   Diana Ross?

GLADYS   Debatable. La La. Where have you been? Don't
                you read the paper? Watch the news?
                Eavesdrop on the bus?

LA LA   Why? All you hear about is whose dead, dying
                or gettin' shot at. If I want to hear a crock of
                shit, all I have to do is sit here and listen to all
                of you going off about this that and the other.
                No thank you. I listen to my records, read my
                old reviews and fan mail and once in a while I
                slip into one of my old costumes and do a tune
                or two. Then I go into the kitchen, make myself
                an egg salad sandwich, cut it into fours, climb
                into bed and have dinner with Ramone. Just the
                two of us. Nice and comfortable and safe.

GLADYS   Are you telling me that you are so scared of
                the world around you that all you do is spend
                time in the past and share meals with a cat
                named Ramone?

LA LA   No. I come here. I sit with my friends, watch the
                people in the park, and wonder about them as

they pass by. For instance. You see that young
man over there? His name is Jim. He is on his
way to his job as an accountant. He'll sit at his
desk all day and think about the girl sitting
across from him, too scared to say hello. He
has become bitter and self-loathing and
someday will commit a series of grizzly crimes
based on a mindless incident, such as someone
pushing past him in the subway. He has one
friend named Ted, who by the way is imaginary,
and he hasn't done his dishes in six months.

(GLADYS *stares at* LA LA *with a disturbed look
on her face.*)

GLADYS   I think you'd better stand up. Your brain is not
getting enough oxygen. (*A beat as* LA LA *looks
at her, perplexed.*) You've been sitting on it
too long. LaLa. What about all those years of
performing? The people. The applause. The
parties. You were surrounded by your fans.
You weren't afraid then.

(LA LA *gets up from the bench, nervously
wringing her hands. She faces the audience as
she speaks.*)

LA LA   I'm not afraid. I just like the world I lived in
better than the world that everyone else is
living in. I was sheltered from everything bad
back in those days, Gladys. My parents, then
my agents, my lovers . . . everyone was so
careful not to let anything crack that
champagne coloured bubble I was living in.
Then, one day it shattered and I had the
breakdown, suddenly all those people that were
protecting me were gone, one by one. Over the
years they either died or moved on with their
lives. All of them would say the same thing just
before they left, 'Hang on in there Carmichael,
it'll happen for ya'. Or 'Hey, you still got it in
ya. Don't give up'. Well I didn't. And I won't.
It's just that the rest of the world never got the
press release saying that La La Carmichael was

back in town. And if they did, they weren't
paying attention. They weren't paying
attention because they were watching *CNN* 24-
7. It's too much to fight with. Sometimes I feel
like David facing Goliath. The only problem is
that I have my slingshot, but I can't find my
rock. And without that rock I can't win, I have
nothing to fight with.

(LA LA *returns to the bench. Her head hangs
low.* GLADYS *reaches over, taking her hand.*)

GLADYS   When my husband told me that he wanted us
to go the rest home, do you know what I said
to him? I said to him that even though it seems
that the world has turned it's back on us,
doesn't mean that we should do the same. It
was then that I realized that we had not just
grown older, we had grown apart. You might
think that the noise of the world is too loud. I
think that the silence is more deafening. If the
sun isn't shining . . . God damnit . . . turn on a
light. Don't just sit there in the dark waiting for
a knock on the door from you-know-who.

LA LA   You're right, Gladys. It's not over till the fat
lady sings. (*A beat. A light bulb goes on in*
LA LA's *head.*) Oh! That's it! I'll call Ella!

GLADYS   La La . . .

LA LA   I know.

BOTH   Dead.

(*The lights fade out.*)

Scene Seven

*Time: Morning. Place: The bench. Setting: Leaves on the
ground herald the passing of the season. The bench is empty.*
LA LA *appears, looking around.*

LA LA   Well. That's three days in a row. No one shows up and you're here alone again. (*She looks around, pointing out people to herself.*) There's that serial killer again. Oh, and that poor girl who was just fired from her job. (*She stops, realizing what she is doing.*) Jesus La La, don't you listen to anyone? Gladys is right. I had a lot of great years. Plenty of sunshine and joy. Poor Eva. Wherever she is, I hope she realizes that the four-letter word for wasted time is fear. Because fear of life can be so much worse than the fear of death. And Anna, oh Anna, you were right. To love and be loved, that is what matters in life.

                  (*She looks over at the rest of the empty bench. She touches the spot where* ROSE *last sat.*)

                  Rose, such a rose. Blooming in silence. Beauty undefined by time, yet withered by the inhumanity of human ignorance.

                  (*She looks around.*)

                  My father always said that if the dog had never stopped to take that shit in the woods, he never would have caught the rabbit in the bushes. Well, you served your purpose, you rickety old bench. Thank you.

                  (LA LA *gets up, dusting off the bench. A* HANDSOME GENTLEMAN *in a dark suit walks up to her and hands her a handkerchief as she brushes the dirt from the bench.*)

MAN   Please, use this, Miss Carmichael.

                  (LA LA *is taken aback.*)

LA LA   How did you know my name?

MAN   You are LaLa Carmichael the jazz singer, aren't you?

LA LA   Yes. Well I used to be. (*She straightens up with self-confidence.*) No . . . no, I *am* La La Carmichael, the jazz singer.

MAN   I got your letter.

LA LA   What letter?

MAN   This one.

          (*He pulls out the letter, handing it to her. She looks down at the address. She looks up at him. LA LA is shaken, she sits down.*)

LA LA   (*puzzled*) Gladys told me that you were . . . well, she said twenty years ago you . . .

MAN   Well, she should know. I mean she has . . . passed on as well.

          (LA LA *becomes frightened.*)

LA LA   How long ago?

MAN   Three months ago.

LA LA   Three months? But what about Rose?

MAN   Two months ago, in her sleep. And Eva six weeks ago. Anna a week later. We had a time trying to get Eva to come. She kept running. Once she met all of you, her fears seemed to dissipate. She's with the rest of them.

LA LA   But . . . how . . . they were all just here last week. I don't understand.

MAN   Ms Carmichael. Look around you. What do you see?

LA LA   A park. People. Trees.

MAN   No. Look harder.

(LA LA *looks around as everything starts to fade away, the stage around them falls dark. She becomes nervous.*)

LA LA   (*frightened*) Please, explain this to me. Are you telling me that I'm . . .

(*Pause.*)

MAN   . . . not in the park. You haven't been for months. All of you have been in . . . well, let's just say you've been waiting for your turn. I'm sorry we didn't come for you sooner. We needed to set a few things up first.

LA LA   (*nervous*) What do you mean 'a few things?'

(*The lights fade. An old fashioned microphone rises from centre stage. A spotlight gleams over it. The man walks LA LA over to the microphone.*)

MAN   Your coat, Ms Carmichael.

(LA LA *removes her coat, handing it to the man. To her amazement she is wearing a beautiful beaded performance dress. He hands her a pair of diamond ear clips from his vest pocket, kisses her on the cheek and walks over to the microphone. She puts them on as he announces her to the audience.*)

MAN   Ladies and gentleman, the William Morris Agency in association with Rainbow and Stars is proud to announce the long awaited return of a legend in the music industry. Miss LaLa Carmichael.

(*He exits. Song – Miss Otis Regrets. During the second verse,* GLADYS, ANNA, ROSE *and* EVA *return in matching dresses and boas to sing/ dance backup for* LA LA, *a-la 'The Supremes'.*)

Miss Otis regrets she's unable to lunch today,
Madam,
Miss Otis regrets she's unable to lunch today.
She is sorry to be delayed,
But last evening down in Lover's Lane she
strayed, Madam,
Miss Otis regrets she's unable to lunch today.

When she woke up and found
That her dream of love was gone, Madam,
She ran to the man
Who had led her so far astray,
And from under her velvet gown
She drew a gun and shot her lover down,
Madam,
Miss Otis regrets she's unable to lunch today.

When the mob came and got her
And dragged her from the jail, Madam,
They strung her upon
The old willow across the way,
And the moment before she died
She lifted up her lovely head and cried, Madam,
"Miss Otis regrets she's unable to lunch today."

(Blackout. End of Act One.)

ACT TWO

Scene One

Music in as the house lights fade out, 'Get Happy'.

Time: Eternity. Place: Heaven. Setting: Looking very much like the previous set, with the exception of the fact that everything, including the grass, is bright white. In essence, it is the same area of park we have been in, except now, since in heaven, everything is white and the New York City skyline has gone. (NB: costumes for the cast are still as they were. No white robes.) ANNA *enters with* ROSE *on her arm. She is waving to someone off stage.*

ANNA   Goodbye Jackie. Nice meeting you Mother Theresa (*To* ROSE.) They were so nice.

ROSE   (*abruptly*) Yeah swell. Now lets see if we can find the others. This place is bigger than Giants Stadium, and more crowded, too.

ANNA   I know. I didn't think there would be this many people up here.

ROSE   If there's this many up here, imagine how many are down there.

ANNA   Oh no! You don't think Gladys ended up . . .

                (GLADYS *enters.*)

GLADYS   That Gladys what?

                (ROSE *and* ANNA *throw open their arms. They all hug.*)

ROSE   When we didn't see you, well . . .

GLADYS   Have you seen anyone else?

ROSE   I ran into Bette Davis in the smoking lounge.

GLADYS   There's a smoking lounge?

ANNA   And a salad bar. It's five miles long, with everything you could possibly want.

GLADYS   Oh great. There goes my waistline.

ROSE   You're dead, you don't have to worry about that any more.

ANNA   Oh, Rose, please stop reminding me of that. I don't like to think of it as death. I want to think of this as a long vacation. Kind of like a Carnival Cruise.

GLADYS   Hey, has anyone seen Eva?

ANNA   No. What could she be doing?

GLADYS   Don't know. So, what do we do?

              (*They all look at each other, puzzled. They look around.* GLADYS *spots a bench.*)

GLADYS   Well, why not?

              (*They walk over to the bench and sit down. They look around . . . then at each other . . . something is not right. None of them are in their usual spots. They get up, shift seats to their usual places and sit back down.*)

GLADYS   Rose. I never knew you could sing.

ROSE   I can't. I did like I used to in choir. I mouthed the words.

ANNA   (*to* GLADYS) You were off key.

GLADYS   Was not. I sung like a bird.

ROSE   Yeah, an Ostrich.

LA LA	(*entering*) You all stunk, that's why I never had La-lettes.
ANNA/ GLADYS/ ROSE	La La!
ROSE	Get your butt over here.
ANNA	What have you been doing? We've been looking all over for you?
LA LA	I had choir practise. You should see who's in there. It's like show time at the Apollo all over again. Duke, Ella, Benny, Glen, they're all here.
ROSE	Josephine?
LA LA	No! I truly am in heaven.
ANNA	Last night before bed, someone stopped by my room, tucked me in and told me a bedtime story. He was a little odd. The story was, too.
GLADYS	What was his name?
ANNA	Edgar . . . or Allen . . . I forget. He kept going on and on and on about a heart or something. I pretended to nod right off at the very beginning, so that he would go. I think he snuck in here.
LA LA	No one sneaks into heaven.
GLADYS	(*pointing to the audience*) Then how do you explain him?
LA LA	That's not Hitler. That's Charlie Chaplin.
GLADYS	I know its Charlie Chaplin. That's why I asked.

(*From behind them comes a sweet-looking older man* (NUNZIO), *dressed in a three-piece grey pinstripe suit. He stands, quietly smiling at them.*)

ANNA   You know, just because you've had a few indiscretions in your life doesn't mean you have to go . . . well . . . to –

GLADYS   To Hell? Say it, Anna. Go-to-Hell.

ANNA   No. I will not say it. Not here. Of all places. (*She stops, sensing something.*)

GLADYS   Sweety, what is it?

ANNA   I don't know . . . (*Turning around slowly.*) It's just a warm . . . (*Spotting the man.*) Nunzio?

NUNZIO   Hello Anna.

(*She gets off the bench, rushes over to him. She stops for a moment just before reaching him and they share a long tender hug. They break their embrace, then, embrace again.*)

LA LA   Mmm. You go, girl.

ANNA   Oh, Nunzio. I missed you so much. Let me look at you. How handsome you look in that suit.

NUNZIO   It was always your favourite.

ANNA   You accepted your award in it. You were so happy. That's why I had you buried in it. (*Loving.*) Oh, look at you.

(GLADYS *jumps up.*)

GLADYS   Wait a minute. Are you telling me that I have to go through eternity in this dress?

ROSE   (*snickering*) And those shoes.

LA LA   Oh, get over it Feinberg.

GLADYS	I hate this dress. It's loud, unflattering and well . . .
ROSE	Just like it's owner.
GLADYS	Oh, go to . . .

(EVA *enters. Only* ANNA *and* NUNZIO *spot her.*)

ANNA	Eva!

(*Everyone turns.*)

EVA	You need a map to get round this place. I told you I was being followed and none of you believed me.
ROSE	You were right Eva. It was death following you.
EVA	Actually, it was Alfred Hitchcock.
GLADYS	Same thing.
EVA	I have someone I want you to meet. Richard dear, come over here.

(RICHARD, *dressed in a black turtleneck, wool trousers and a sport coat, enters. He is still clutching the aforementioned strappy sandal in his hand. He will carry it through the rest of the story as part of his penance.*)

LA LA	He is handsome. Nice catch, Eva.
GLADYS	You don't by any chance have the other one with you?
ANNA	Shhh. Don't mention her!
GLADYS	I'm not talking about her, I'm talking about the shoe. It'll go great with this dress.
ANNA	This is my husband, Nunzio. Nunzio, this is Mr Reisch.

NUNZIO	(*to* ANNA) The one with the floozy? How did he end up?
ANNA	Sshhh. The Lord forgives.
EVA	(*overhearing*) But I haven't.

(*She pulls on his hand, tugging him off stage.*)

EVA	We're having lunch in twenty minutes with Queen Elizabeth I and I want to freshen up. Come along, Richard.

(RICHARD *pauses, about to speak.*)

EVA	(*off stage*) Richard!

(RICHARD *exits.*)

ANNA	Lunch sounds good. Nunzio, there's a buffet that you can't imagine.
NUNZIO	Oh, yes I can. And you would be proud of me. I finally convinced Mamma Cass to try cottage cheese. (*To* GLADYS, ROSE *and* LA LA.) Come on. Let's go and pig out.

(*Everyone heads offstage.* LA LA *goes back for her purse. She turns to catch up with the others when a handsome young black man in his 20s, dressed in 50s clothing, enters.* LA LA *stops dead in her tracks.*)

LA LA	Tuffy? Tuffy Buchanan? As I live and breathe!

(*Blackout.*)

Scene Two

Time: Eternity. Place: Heaven. Setting: The park. LA LA *and* TUFFY *are sitting on a bench, holding hands.*

LA LA   All I kept picturing was you lying there. Your
               poor little body in the street. So still. I kept
               saying, 'Come on Tuffy, tough it out'.

TUFFY   It was a huge truck. Trust me, even you
               couldn't have stopped it. I felt bad for you.
               You spent so much time soul-searching for
               reasons why I was gone, you forgot all the
               reasons why you were living.

LA LA   That's not true. Well, okay, maybe partly true.
               But, I went on. Still, in my heart, I might as well
               have been lying there six feet under with you.
               It wasn't until years later when I met Charlie
               that things seemed a whole lot less grim, for a
               while anyway. I thought he was so strong that
               he could carry the weight of the world in one
               hand and all my sorrow in the other, without
               even breakin' a sweat. But Charlie had other
               things on his mind. He wanted to take care of
               me all right. Take care of me right out of my
               career.

TUFFY   How any man could want to deny you the thing
               you love most? (*He touches her cheek.*)

LA LA   You never were the jealous type. And it wasn't
               Charlie who took away the thing I love most. It
               was Peppy's produce truck.

TUFFY   Well, that was along time ago and it's all in the
               past. (*He reaches into his pocket.*) They buried
               me with this. I was on my way to get the clasp
               fixed for you when . . . well . . . here. (*He
               produces a locket, hangs it around her neck.*)
               Open it.

               (*She complies. Seeing the contents; a picture
               of him and her mother, she smiles.*)

LA LA   Mama was so beautiful. And look at you.
               (*Laughing.*) That little head and those big ears.

TUFFY   Hey. They're not big.

LA LA   Oh no? Mama used to say that giving birth to you was like trying to push a tricycle through a pea shooter . . . backwards! (*Laughs.*) But you were the most beautiful baby boy we'd ever seen. And I would have done anything to keep you safe from harm. When I told Mama that we were moving to the city together, she fought me tooth and nail.

TUFFY   I remember sitting up in my room, bags packed, listening to you two battle it out. She said, 'You can't even take care of your rag doll, how are you going to take care of a fifteen year old boy?' That's when you said, 'I'm not taking care of him Mama, we're gonna take care of each other'.

LA LA   (*with a bit of regret*) Then I told her that she would never have to worry about anything happening to you, because I would never let it happen.

TUFFY   And you didn't. I had eight wonderful years. I met Mimi and got to play saxophone along side you in every speakeasy up and down the Broadway strip. I would have made it to the Apollo but . . .

LA LA   Let's not talk about it any more.

(GLADYS *enters.*)

GLADYS   Talk about what?

LA LA   Gladys, this is my brother Tuffy. Tuffy Buchanan, this is Gladys Feinberg.

TUFFY   (*to* LA LA) Feinberg?

LA LA   Times have changed.

TUFFY   Pleased to meet you. Any friend of my sister's is a friend of mine.

GLADYS   You never mentioned a brother?

LA LA   Yes I did.

GLADYS   No, you didn't. You may have mentioned
              'brothers' but never *a* brother.

LA LA   So what are you going to do, kill me? Have you
              seen anyone you know yet?

GLADYS   (*mopy*) No. All alone. Surrounded by
              thousands of souls, yet all alone.

TUFFY   Well, you can hang out with us.

LA LA   You're awfully mopy. What's up? You've
              always been so full of piss and vinegar?

GLADYS   I don't know. It's like something has happened.
              I can't explain it.

TUFFY   Try. It helps to talk it out.

GLADYS   Oh, why bother. I got all eternity to wander
              around. Don't worry about me.

              (ANNA *enters with* NUNZIO.)

NUNZIO   (*to* ANNA) For a dead girl, you can surely pack
              it away. (*To everyone.*) I've never seen her eat
              so much in all my years.

ANNA   I was trying to conserve. We weren't the
              richest couple on the block. We had to be
              careful. Plus gluttony is a sin.

NUNZIO   Well then I'm a sinner, cause I'm a glutton for
              your kisses.

ANNA   Nunzio, hush. Saint Ignacious is standing right
              over there. I don't think he'd appreciate your
              PDA.

NUNZIO   PDA?

ANNA   Public Display of Affection.

GLADYS   Where's Rose?

ANNA   She went off looking for Shirley. Said
             something about checking the library. She'll be
             by later. Well, what do you say we take a load
             off?

             (ANNA *and* NUNZIO *sit on one bench,* LA LA *and*
             TUFFY *sit down on the other,* GLADYS *by* LA LA'S
             side.)

GLADYS   The weather here is beautiful. I haven't seen
             weather like this since Marvin and I were on
             our honeymoon in Capri. Boy, that was a
             beautiful place. (*To the sky.*) No offence, this is
             pure heaven, but Capri had palm trees and pina
             coladas. (*Back to the bench.*) He was so
             handsome. He had this shock of dark wavy hair
             and these blue eyes that reflected the colour of
             the Mediterranean waters. And when he smiled,
             oh when he smiled – well, Cary Grant would
             have been jealous. (*Fondly, with a bit of lust.*)
             I remember the first time I saw him in a
             swimsuit. (*To* LA LA.) PS: *From Here to
             Eternity* was just a hop, skip and jump.

LA LA   Hello!

             (LA LA *leans in closer, getting into* GLADYS'
             story.)

GLADYS   Remember that stable boy you used to dream
             about? He had his horse parked in my barn six
             nights a week.

LA LA   Sweet Jesus!!!

             (*A voice offstage answers . . . 'YES?' Everyone
             does a double-take.*)

ANNA   (*flustered*) I don't think we should be
              discussing such things here.

LA LA   Button it, Cinzano. I want to hear the rest of
              this story. Tuffy, cover your ears. (*Eagerly.*)
              Go on, Gladys . . .

GLADYS   So this one night, the last night of our
              honeymoon, we're on the balcony at the hotel.
              There was soft blues wafting over the trees in
              the distance and the lights from the village
              below were twinkling in the limpid pools of his
              eyes . . .

TUFFY   Barbara Cartland, eat your heart out.

GLADYS   And he takes me in his arms, looks me in the
              eyes and says . . .

              (MARVIN *enters behind her.*)

MARVIN   Are you gonna tell that damn story for the rest
              of eternity? Because if you are, then this must
              be hell.

              (*She turns, in shock and a bit angry.*)

GLADYS   Marvin Feinberg!!! What did you do, pay off
              Saint Peter at the gate?

MARVIN   Is that any way to treat a man who nodded off
              during his favourite episode of *Gilligan's
              Island* and never woke up?

GLADYS   You're right Marvin, I should be more
              sensitive. After all, you did suffer a terrible
              blow. Here, let me comfort you.

              (*She gets up, goes over to him and gives him a
              hug.*)

MARVIN   OWWW! (*Pulling away.*) You bit my ear!

GLADYS   You don't need 'em! You never listened anyway. Oh, by the way . . . they NEVER get off the island. Just like you never got out of that chair. You're just sore cause I beat you up here.

MARVIN   No, I'm sore that your family buried me in this ratty old sweater.

GLADYS   Oh, and this Mu-mu you picked out for me is supposed to be flattering? I feel like an extra from *The Lion King*.

TUFFY   (*trying to flatter*) Actually, I think it's very pretty. You look like an . . . Island Princess.

GLADYS   (*to* MARVIN) Now, that's how you give a compliment.

MARVIN   No. That's how you shovel a load of crap. You should know, Gladys. That's what are whole marriage was. You on one side shovelling and me on the other. And finally we got the pile so high we couldn't see or hear each other any more. You think all I did in that rest home was watch *Wheel of Fortune* and eat applesauce? No. I sat there and thought about our life. And you know what I think? Maybe we were better off living like that. Because my life was fine and your life was fine, but our life was one big pile of . . .

(NUNZIO *breaks in.*)

NUNZIO   Please. Please. Don't say anything you'll regret. You've both had a shock. It'll be alright once you get settled in. Don't worry, you'll see, the more time you spend here, the more . . .

GLADYS   The more I'll realize what a fool I was all my life. But you know what, I'm not gonna make the same mistake twice. I may have spent my life with you, but I'd rather spend eternity alone.

ANNA   (*flustered*) Please, settle down. Nunzio, take
                Marvin to the bocci court, talk to him.

MARVIN   (*to* GLADYS) Oh really. What do you mean by
                that?

ANNA   She just means she needs some time . . .
                (GLADYS *cuts in.*) . . . to get her thoughts
                together.

GLADYS   I don't need any more time, I know what I want.

MARVIN   What? What do you want?

GLADYS   I WANT A DIVORCE!!

MARVIN   FINE!

LA LA   You can't get a divorce.

GLADYS   Why not?

LA LA   Because there are no lawyers in heaven!

                (*Blackout.*)

Scene Three

Time: Eternity. Place: Heaven. Setting: The park. ROSE *and*
SHIRLEY *are on the bench.* SHIRLEY *is reading a book.*

SHIRLEY   Here's one. (*Reciting.*)
                Squirrel squirrel on the ground,
                You don't make a single sound.
                I know why so still you are,
                You've been run over by a car. (*She laughs.*)

ROSE   Shirley! That's sick.

SHIRLEY   No. That's funny.

ROSE   Maybe in your warped little mind. Oh, how I
            missed you. I'd forgotten about all those
            Sundays that we would sit around the
            apartment and you would read to me from the
            paper.

SHIRLEY   And you would drink that Mexican coffee. The
            smell alone could give you a buzz. Whatever
            happened to Mirabelle?

ROSE   Last time I saw her she was still on the window
            sill, staring out at the street. I hope she's okay.

SHIRLEY   That cat never liked me.

ROSE   Nonsense. She loved you. After you died, she
            sat in your chair for weeks and wouldn't let
            anyone come near it. Not even me. I used to sit
            on the floor next to it and listen hard as I
            could, just trying to hear your voice. Never did.

SHIRLEY   Do you remember the night you woke up and
            thought you felt someone sitting next to you?
            It was me. They let me out for twenty minutes.
            They said I wasn't supposed to let you know I
            was there, but I knew you could feel me in the
            room.

ROSE   Why you little . . .

SHIRLEY   You were so funny. The first thing you did was
            get out that locket from under your nightie and
            stare at my picture. If you had looked up and
            hard enough you probably could have seen me.

ROSE   I remember thinking, one more hour, just one
            more hour.

SHIRLEY   Well, now we have an hour that never ends.

ROSE   Why did it have to happen? I tried to figure it
            out over a hundred times. Why would God let
            people like that do things like that? It just isn't
            right.

SHIRLEY   Rose. Let me tell you something that I've learnt
             up here. God makes all kinds of people in this
             world. A balance, if you will. There will always
             be good in the world. And the bad people
             weren't born bad, they learned, or maybe
             because they never learned they ended up that
             way. You can make certain choices, but if no
             one gives you an option, then you take what
             you can get.

ROSE   Are you asking me to feel sorry for those
             people that beat you up and left you for dead
             in the street?

SHIRLEY   No, but the lessons we learn in life and the
             hand that we're dealt sometimes precludes us
             from playing our cards the right way . . . so that
             everyone wins . . . and when that happens,
             someone loses. Rose . . . Rose, there are times
             when I used to sit and think . . . I still had A, B
             and C to do before I died, so why, why did it
             happen? You know what, obviously A, B and C
             were not as important as L, O, V, and E. And
             that I did accomplish. (*Taking her hand.*) With
             great results.

             (ROSE *takes* SHIRLEY'S *hand to her cheek, looks
             into her eyes. There is a loving silence. Then
             from offstage . . .*)

GLADYS   I don't know what you expect me to say to that,
             but I can tell you one thing, if we weren't dead
             already, I'd kill myself just to get away from
             you!!

             (GLADYS *storms on stage, sits down on the
             opposite bench, arms crossed.*)

ROSE   Hello Gladys? You and Marvin having another
             . . . fight?

GLADYS   Another? We never finished the first one. (*To
             SHIRLEY.*) Who are you?

ROSE   Gladys, this is Shirley.

GLADYS   (*with recognition*) Oh yeah, I recognize your
              picture. Let me tell you something, you people
              have the right idea.

SHIRLEY   You people?

GLADYS   Yeah, You people. Lebanese.

ROSE   Les-bi-an, Gladys, Les-bi-an.

GLADYS   Whatever. (*Gets up, moves to* SHIRLEY'S *side,
              sits down.*) You got it made. No man to clean
              up after. No smelly cigars and football games . .
              . I think I might join you. Is it too late to sign
              up? Is there an initiation fee?

ROSE   Gladys, you don't sign up . . .

              (MARVIN *barrels on stage.*)

MARVIN   I wasn't through talking . . . don't walk out on
              me when I'm talking to you.

GLADYS   Oh, was that me you were talking to? Well
              whatever you've got to say, it's too late.

MARVIN   Why?

GLADYS   (*hanging an arm around* SHIRLEY'S *shoulder*)
              Because, I'm becoming a lesbian. Shirley and
              Rose and I are moving to a log cabin and we're
              going to make pottery together . . . and drink
              beer and make . . . wood carvings of Germanic
              figures with Swiss army knives. (*Pulling a
              knife out of her pocket.*) See?

MARVIN   Where did you get that?

GLADYS   Joan Crawford dropped it in the cafeteria.

MARVIN   Stealing in heaven!

ROSE   How did Joan Crawford get in?

SHIRLEY   Please, suffering through the making of *Baby
                Jane* with Bette Davis is penance enough for
                anyone.

MARVIN   Listen. Maybe Anna and Nunzio were right.
                Maybe now . . . up here, we can make things
                better. Maybe that's why we were brought
                back together.

                (GLADYS *rises*.)

GLADYS   No. You were brought here to torture me for all
                eternity because God couldn't think of any
                better way to amuse himself since Bush got
                into office.

                (*She storms off. Blackout.*)

                        Scene Four

Time: Eternity. Place: Heaven. Setting: TUFFY *sits alone on a
bench, playing blues on his harmonica. He plays for a couple
of minutes, uninterrupted, until* MARVIN *enters.* MARVIN *stands
watching and listening, as if he were remembering a happy
moment in his life. He smiles, clearing his throat.*

MARVIN   I thought you people played harps?

TUFFY   They were out of harps. Tiny Tim got the last
                one. Besides, nothing beats the sound of the
                blues. Where's the rest of the Bnai Brith Brady
                Bunch?

MARVIN   Say, what have you got against me?

TUFFY   Me? Nothing. (*Pause.*) I just think, well, I used
                to think that people should stick together. It
                makes them stronger.

MARVIN   Sometimes when people stick together, someone ends up left out. You can't assume that if you are one way that everyone who is like that will always go along with you. And you shouldn't just shut the door on someone because of what they look like.

TUFFY   Well, when I was alive, things were different. All someone had to do was look at you and decide you were no good.

MARVIN   I have news for you son, I come from that same time. The only difference is that I lived long enough to see that time come to an end. Well, almost to an end. You and I have a lot more in common than you think. They burned your church down in the Atlanta when you were twelve years old. Isn't that right?

TUFFY   How did you know?

MARVIN   La La told me. Well, our synagogue was bombed and pillaged for the exact same reason. But you know what, you can question a person's existence . . . but you shouldn't condemn it. Just like you can test a person's faith . . . but you can't burn it to the ground.

TUFFY   La La used to say she wanted to he a famous radio star, because then all anyone would hear is her voice, not see her colour. Do you know how much that hurt?

MARVIN   Look around, Tuffy. You see where you are. Heaven, and there is no hurt in heaven. So don't bring it up here, because there's no room.

TUFFY   Have you told that to Gladys?

MARVIN   Gladys is a tough old broad. This has been going on between us for a long time.

TUFFY   You're gonna be up here for eternity. Maybe
               it's time for you to come around. Maybe you
               should remind her that there is no hurt in
               heaven. My Mimi and I were together for six
               years and we fought all the time. But we never
               went to bed angry.

MARVIN   If that were our rule, we wouldn't have slept for
               twenty years. I just can't communicate with
               her. I try. But every time I open my mouth, all I
               taste is shoe leather.

TUFFY   Then maybe you shouldn't say anything. Just
               do something to show her how you feel, cause
               you obviously can't tell her.

MARVIN   Like what?

               (RICHARD *enters.*)

RICHARD   How about flowers? No matter what I did
               wrong, if I sent Eva flowers, everything got
               better.

MARVIN   From what I hear, your apartment must have
               looked like a funeral home.

RICHARD   Hey! I went to my grave loving my wife.

TUFFY   And your mistress?

RICHARD   What is this heaven, or Melrose Place? How
               did you know . . .

MARVIN   What else have we got to do all day but
               gossip? That bocci court is a hotbed of
               information. Nunzio is worse than Anna when it
               comes to telling other people's stories. He's
               Hans Christian Anderson and Sidney Sheldon
               rolled into one.

RICHARD   Well, no matter. After all, we made it up here.
               So I guess there's no harm in airing out a little
               dirty laundry. Is it true Gladys kicked you out?

MARVIN   Yeah, I'm just kind of floatin' around right now
            . . . a free spirit. I kind of like it.

TUFFY   He's lying. He's miserable. So, Richard . . . got
            any other suggestions for the fiddler without a
            roof?

RICHARD   You need to do something that only you know
            she really likes. That way, you'll show her all
            over again that you care. Women love it when
            you try to redeem yourself. It gives them a
            sense of security. Do something romantic . . .
            dashing . . . dangerous.

MARVIN   This is Marvin Feinberg you're talking to, not
            James Bond.

RICHARD   I'm not saying that you need to make a bomb
            out of a bobby pin and a bunch of toothpicks.
            Just do something small. (*He pauses.*) When
            Eva came home after she had lost the baby, she
            was so distant, I thought she'd never come
            back. Then I went out and got her a puppy. Not
            that Willy replaced the baby . . . but Eva lit up
            like the Rockefeller Centre Christmas tree when
            she saw him.

GLADYS   (*thinking hard*) A puppy. Where do I get a
            puppy?

RICHARD   . . . I'm not saying a puppy. The point of the
            puppy story is to do something that you know
            will touch her in a way only you can.

            (MARVIN *rises from the bench.*)

MARVIN   (*with conviction*) I'll do it, or die trying . . .

RICHARD   You're dead already!

MARVIN   Good. This takes the pressure off.

TUFFY   There's the spirit.

(Marvin *exits with determination.*)

TUFFY   Do you think he can do it?

RICHARD   I hope so. Eternity will feel like . . . well,
           eternity if he can't.

TUFFY   There's a good reason to play the blues.

           (Tuffy *lifts the harmonica to his mouth, plays
           softly, lost in the moment.* Richard *digs his
           hand into his pocket.*)

RICHARD   (*to* Tuffy) You wana see Willy?

TUFFY   (*becoming flustered*) What? I . . . I think I hear
           La La calling, I gotta go.

           (*He exits.* Richard *pulls out a picture of Willy,
           tries to show him. Too late, he's gone.* Richard
           continues . . . to the picture.)

RICHARD   I realized too late that the you were really a
           way to alleviate my guilt for cheating on Eva. I
           loved her so much and I still do. But, when you
           make the same mistake over and over again,
           after a while the mistake becomes a routine part
           of your life and then . . . then after a while you
           just keep making it, because you start to think
           that it is all you know how to do. Which is
           harder? Living with regrets, or dying from
           them. You can't change regrets after you're
           gone. (*Looking around.*) Up here . . . well here
           you just thank God that you can't create new
           ones. And that is one, perfect, concept of
           heaven.

           (Eva *comes on stage. She has been listening
           from the wings all along.*)

EVA   How could you do such a thing? I could just –

RICHARD   Kill me?

EVA   Well . . . yes.

RICHARD   I don't know. Do you remember last winter?
             That horrible storm we had?

EVA   The one where Willy got lost in the snow and
             you had to go find him?

RICHARD   And do you remember how worried you got
             because as I got further and further from the
             house you could barely see me through the
             storm?

EVA   Yes, but –

RICHARD   That's how I felt. It's like my head was a snow
             globe. And you and our life together was in the
             middle of it. It was always right there in the
             centre. My life with you was as crystal clear as
             that globe. But then things got so busy, so
             hectic, so out of control that the globe got all
             shaken up and the snow was swirling around
             so fast that I couldn't find you.

EVA   But you found her.

RICHARD   I guess I should have waited for the storm to
             settle, but I was so cold and . . .

EVA   No, I was so cold. After the baby –

RICHARD   Don't say it.

EVA   Died . . . the baby died, Richard. And part of me
             went with it. That's the part you were looking
             for in the storm.

             (*Taking her hand.*)

RICHARD   Have I found it now?

EVA   And you'll never lose it again.

(RICHARD *and* EVA *kiss. He dips her. The shoe knocks her in the back of the head.*)

EVA   Richard, get rid of that shoe before I put it somewhere even God doesn't shine his holy light!

(RICHARD *tosses the shoe offstage. They laugh and kiss passionately again. Blackout.*)

Scene Five

Time: Eternity. Place: Heaven. Setting: GLADYS, ANNA *and* NUNZIO *sit on the bench.* GLADYS *is doing a crossword puzzle.* ANNA *and* NUNZIO *are sitting next to her, holding hands.*

NUNZIO   . . . So, then Maria turns to me and says, 'The next time you decide to go and see clients, take the lucky clove of garlic out of your pocket. What ever happened her?

ANNA   The last time I saw her I was in Balducci's. She's well, living with her husband in their apartment in the village. She looked just as lovely.

NUNZIO   (*kissing her hand*) True love will do that for you.

GLADYS   So that explains my cottage cheese thighs and jowls?

ANNA   Gladys. You know that you and Marvin could be happy. It's just that neither of you want to bend.

GLADYS   Bend? Bend? I've bent over backwards for him more times than Elizabeth Taylor on her honeymoons. He's the one suffering from rigger mortis of the mind.

Nunzio	The two of you are stubborn. Why not try a little hanky panky? You know, a smooch here and there.
Gladys	I didn't think they allowed dirty old men in heaven.
Nunzio	They don't. Only dirty old married men. There's a difference.
Gladys	What?
Nunzio	Dirty old married men are generally married to dirty old women.
Anna	Excuse me?
Nunzio	(*with a naughty smile*) Anna? Saturday night linguine?
Anna	Well, maybe a bit. (*Snickering.*) But you have to admit, it's a whole lot better when your pasta's al dente.
	(*They share a laugh.*)
Gladys	All right Mama Celestial, it's a little early in the day for this. I haven't even had my coffee.
	(Marvin *enters with two cups of coffee in hand.*)
Marvin	Why not, there's a Starbucks on every other cloud.
	(*He walks over to her. She goes back to her puzzle, ignoring him.*)
Gladys	(*to the puzzle*) Rubbish.
Anna	I know . . . a seven-letter word for carelessly discarded things!

would realize that I wasn't the strong man that you fell in love with.

GLADYS   I knew who you were the day we married. I knew that you were a good man, with hopes and dreams, and then you just gave them all up. You closed down the store, sold all our assets and ran into hiding.

(*He stands, pacing.*)

MARVIN   I'm going to tell you something and I want you to listen to me carefully. Do you remember the day I came home and told you that I was selling the store?

GLADYS   November 27th, 1975.

MARVIN   And I wouldn't tell you why exactly.

GLADYS   No, you wouldn't. All you said was, 'I have my reasons. Trust me'. And I did.

MARVIN   Now I am going to tell you. (*Hesitating.*) Ronnie Leibman came looking for a hammer. A ball peen hammer. There was none on the floor, so I went into the back and looked for one. Up and down the aisles I went, checking all the boxes. When I came out he was gone.

GLADYS   So he left. What of it?

MARVIN   Wait. When I walked around the corner I saw a man behind the counter. He was prying open the register with a crowbar. I say, 'What are you doing? Stop that'. He raised the crowbar at me . . . (*Mimicking the motion as he speaks.*) So I backed away. I stood there, terrified . . . I thought I was going to have a heart attack on that very spot. (*Pausing . . . pondering.*) He says to me, 'That's right old man, you just stay there and maybe you'll live to see that social security cheque show up in the mail'. After he left I called the police.

GLADYS   So you were robbed. It happens.

MARVIN   That was the fifth time. I couldn't risk a sixth.

                (*He sits down, taking her hand in his.*)

GLADYS   So instead you shut yourself off from me and
                the world? Did you ever stop and think that I
                was robbed too? That you risked losing me?

MARVIN   . . . I didn't intentionally shut myself off from
                you, Gladys. It just happened. I could feel
                myself slipping away, like a sink full of water
                with a tiny crack in its rubber stopper. Drop by
                drop the water slips down the drain and before
                you know it all the water is gone. Then, when I
                finally realized it . . .

GLADYS   (*putting her hand to his lips*) If I don't know
                that something is wrong, how can I help make it
                right? Don't ever be afraid to say what you
                feel, just be afraid if you can't. (*With love.*) Use
                that big mouth of yours for something besides
                eating prunes . . . okay?

                (*She kisses him on the cheek. He looks into
                her eyes, smiling.*)

MARVIN   Here's something else they can do.

                (*He kisses her full on the lips.* SHIRLEY *and*
                ROSE *enter, laughing.*)

SHIRLEY   . . . if it weren't for that railing, I would have
                gone ass over tea kettle right into the water.

                (*They spot* Marvin *and* GLADYS *kissing.*)

ROSE   Gladys? Is that you in that lip lock?

GLADYS   Yeah, it's me. The old smoothie here got to me
                all over again.

ROSE   How'd you do it skipper?

MARVIN   I listened to my heart and my friends.

ROSE   Does this mean we can all rest in peace now?

GLADYS   (*winking at* MARVIN) Well, I don't know how
                much rest we're gonna get.

                (*They kiss again, laughing.* ANNA *and* NUNZIO,
                EVA, RICHARD, TUFFY *and* LA LA *enter. They all
                look at* GLADYS *and* MARVIN.)

LA LA   Praise the Lord!

TUFFY   (*appalled*) And pass the bucket!

ANNA   Oh, it's sweet, Tuffy.

NUNZIO   I knew you could do it.

                (*He sits down on the bench.*)

TUFFY   I guess it was just a matter of time. (*He sits as
                well.*)

SHIRLEY   And a cattle prod. (*She sits.*)

                (ANNA *looks at* LA LA . . . *they eye the bench
                and rush for it. Everyone wedges in
                uncomfortably, nudging each other for elbow
                room.*)

LA LA   Rose . . . move down a little.

ROSE   I would, but the jiggling Gigolo's butt is taking
                up too much room.

EVA   There is nothing wrong with my husband's
                butt!

GLADYS   Other than the fact that it's seen every bed in
                the Waldorf Astoria! (*Ad-libs.*)

Nunzio   That wasn't very nice.

Gladys   Nuts to nice . . . and you! Move down!

     (Anna *rises and fishes through her purse.*)

Anna   (*shouts*) That's it!

     (*She turns to the bench, pulls out the gun . . . everyone reacts, jumping up.*)

Nunzio   Anna! What are you . . .

Anna   Hush, Nunzio. Now everyone, starting with you Gladys, line up . . . boy-girl, boy-girl, girl-girl, boy-girl. (*They comply.*) Now sit. Sit! (*She fires the gun. They drop down on the bench.* Anna, *still standing, blows on the barrel of the gun.*) Good. Now maybe we can get some peace around here.

     (*A dead white dove with an olive branch in its beak falls from the sky, landing with a thud. Everyone stares at the dove.* Anna *turns in horror. Everyone turns their stare to* Anna . . . *they are all in shock.*)

Eva   I guess you found the bullets.

Female Voice   (*over PA system*) Attention everyone. (*Blows into microphone.*) Mrs Anna May Cinzano, please report to the head office. Mrs Anna May Cinzano please report to the head office *immediately!*

Anna   Oh shit!!!

     (*The end.*)